SHARKS BITE, OCTOPUSES ENTANGLE

HUNTER AND HUNTED ⌐ANIMAL SURVIVAL⌐

KIP ALMASY

PowerKiDS press™

New York

Published in 2018 by The Rosen Publishing Group, Inc.
29 East 21st Street, New York, NY 10010

First Edition

Editor: Theresa Morlock
Book Design: Reann Nye

Photo Credits: Cover (shark), p. 17 Ramon Carretero/Shutterstock.com; cover (octopus), p. 1 JonMilnes/Shutterstock.com; p. 4 Matt9122/Shutterstock.com; pp. 5 (whale shark), 15 (whale shark) Krzysztof Odziomek/Shutterstock.com; pp. 5 (red octopus), 11 Rich Carey/Shutterstock.com; pp. 5 (giant Pacific octopus), 22 (octopus) Kondratuk Aleksei/Shutterstock.com; pp. 5 (great white shark), 15 (great white shark) VisionDive/Shutterstock.com; p. 5 (map) pingebat/Shutterstock.com; p. 6 Joel Larsson/Shutterstock.com; p. 7 Vladimir Wrangel/Shutterstock.com; p. 8 dade72/Shutterstock.com; p. 9 John Woodcock/Getty Images; p. 10 Stasis Photo/Shutterstock.com; p. 12 Paranee Hansakul/Shutterstock.com; p. 13 Jurgen Freund/Nature Picture Library/Getty Images; p. 14 Grant M Henderson/Shutterstock.com; p. 15 (dwarf lanternshark) https://commons.wikimedia.org/wiki/File:Etmopterus_perryi_SI_cr.jpg; p. 16 frantisekhojdysz/Shutterstock.com; p. 18 Tomas Kotouc/Shutterstock.com; p. 19 Martin Prochazkacz/Shutterstock.com; p. 20 Willyam Bradberry/Shutterstock.com; p. 21 Vittorio Bruno/Shutterstock.com; p. 22 (shark) Mavenvision/Shutterstock.com.

Cataloging-in-Publication Data

Names: Almasy, Kip.
Title: Sharks bite, octopuses entangle / Kip Almasy.
Description: New York : PowerKids Press, 2018. | Series: Hunter and hunted: animal survival | Includes index.
Identifiers: ISBN 9781508156680 (pbk.) | ISBN 9781508156611 (library bound) | ISBN 9781508156505 (6 pack)
Subjects: LCSH: Sharks-Juvenile literature. | Octopuses-Juvenile literature.
Classification: LCC QL638.9 A46 2018 | DDC 597.3-dc23

Manufactured in the United States of America

CPSIA Compliance Information: Batch Batch #BS17PK: For Further Information contact Rosen Publishing, New York, New York at 1-800-237-9932

CONTENTS

LIFE IN THE OCEAN

Thousands of strange creatures swim through the salty blue waters of Earth's oceans. This mysterious underwater **environment** is populated by a wide variety of species, or kinds, of animals, which range from tiny seahorses to giant blue whales. Octopuses and sharks are two of the most interesting animals of them all.

The shark is a swift killer whose speed and skill are almost unbeatable. The octopus is a sneaky survivor that creeps in the shadows waiting to attack. What happens when these two enemies meet in the wild waters of the ocean?

RED OCTOPUS HABITAT

NORTH
AMERICA

PACIFIC
OCEAN

WHALE SHARK HABITAT

NORTH
AMERICA

EUROPE

ASIA

AFRICA

SOUTH
AMERICA

AUSTRALIA

GREAT WHITE SHARK HABITAT

NORTH
AMERICA

EUROPE

ASIA

AFRICA

SOUTH
AMERICA

AUSTRALIA

GIANT PACIFIC OCTOPUS HABITAT

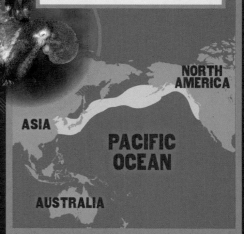

NORTH
AMERICA

ASIA

PACIFIC
OCEAN

AUSTRALIA

Sharks and octopuses live in oceans
around the world. Some live in deep waters
and others prefer waters on the coast.

ODD OCTOPUSES

There are more than 300 species of octopuses living in oceans all over the world. They may be as small as the *Octopus wolfi*, which is about an inch (2.54 cm) long, or as large as the giant Pacific octopus, which can reach 16 feet (4.9 m) long or more.

Octopuses spend most of their time alone. They sometimes build homes called dens, using their arms to stack rocks into place. Octopuses **communicate** with each other by changing color. They can also change the color of their skin to draw attention to themselves or to blend into their surroundings.

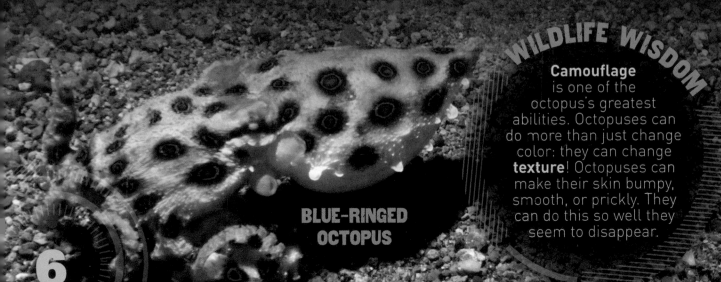

BLUE-RINGED OCTOPUS

WILDLIFE WISDOM

Camouflage is one of the octopus's greatest abilities. Octopuses can do more than just change color: they can change **texture**! Octopuses can make their skin bumpy, smooth, or prickly. They can do this so well they seem to disappear.

Octopuses are famous for their eight tentacles, which are long, thin limbs. Across the 300 or so octopus species, there are many differences in appearance and **behavior**.

WEIRD BODIES

Octopuses are invertebrates, which means they don't have a backbone. They breathe through **gills** on either side of their body. Octopuses have three hearts. Two pump blood through their gills and one pumps blood through their body. When octopuses swim, the third heart stops beating.

To save energy, octopuses usually crawl instead of swim. When they want to move quickly, they use a special body part called a siphon. Octopuses push a jet of water through the siphon to **propel** themselves through the water. When an octopus feels scared, it can shoot a dark liquid called ink from its siphon to confuse an attacker.

WILDLIFE WISDOM

There are many strange things about an octopus's body. Did you know octopus blood is blue instead of red? Or that octopuses don't have ears? Although octopuses are able to change the color of their skin and can identify colors, they don't see them the same way other animals do.

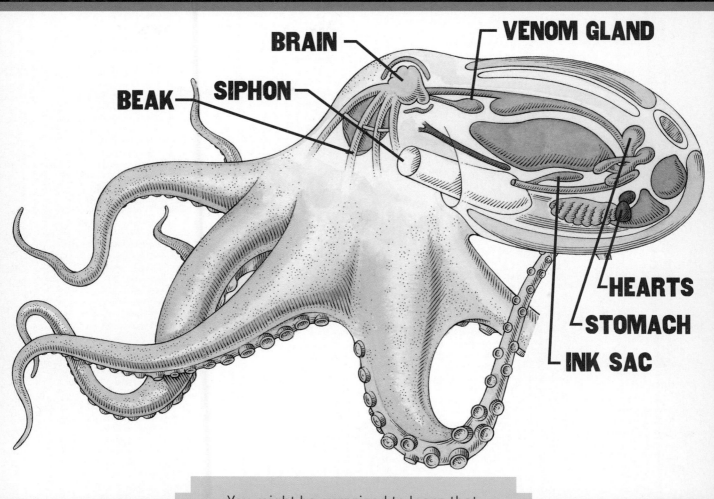

BRAIN

VENOM GLAND

BEAK

SIPHON

HEARTS

STOMACH

INK SAC

You might be surprised to learn that octopuses have beaks! They use their beak to put **venom** into their **prey** and to crush crabs and other animals with shells.

TERRIFIC TENTACLES

Octopus tentacles have **nerves** that allow the tentacles to work independently of the octopus's body. Tentacles that are cut off from the rest of the body can actually continue to move. If an octopus loses a tentacle, it can grow a new one to replace it! This is called regeneration. Octopuses use a special chemical called AChE to rebuild nerves and body structures.

Each of an octopus's eight tentacles has over 200 suckers on it.

An octopus's tentacles are lined with suckers, which help them move and grip things. Octopuses actually taste through their suckers. They use their sense of taste to help them find their prey.

SURPRISE ATTACK!

Octopuses are carnivores, which means they only eat meat. Their diet is mostly made up of crabs, shrimp, lobsters, and other small sea creatures. They also eat other octopuses and sometimes sharks.

One bite from the tiny blue-ringed octopus can kill an adult person within minutes.

Octopuses hunt their prey by using their camouflage to hide in plain sight. They prefer to hunt in dark, cloudy water, using their eyesight to spot prey. Octopuses use their tentacles to **entangle** their prey before biting into it with their sharp beak. When octopuses bite their prey, they put venom into it. The venom paralyzes prey, which means it's unable to move.

13

SHARK BASICS

More than 400 shark species have been discovered. Sharks range in size from the 8-inch (20.3 cm) dwarf lanternshark to the 40-foot (12.2 m) whale shark.

The size of a shark usually depends on what type of environment it lives in. Different shark species live in oceans all over the world. Some of them travel hundreds of miles to seek out food. They live in coastal waters, the deep sea, freshwater, and many other conditions. Sharks spend much of their time alone but sometimes hunt and travel in groups.

BASKING SHARK

WILDLIFE WISDOM

Sharks have been around since before the time of the dinosaurs! The sharks on Earth today came from species that lived over 400 million years ago.

DWARF LANTERNSHARK

GREAT WHITE SHARK

WHALE SHARK

Some shark species could drown if they stop swimming! The great white shark, for example, doesn't have the right muscles to move water through its mouth and over its gills. It needs to swim in order to breathe properly.

SHARK POWERS

Sharks have very highly developed senses. They can smell a single drop of blood in 10 billion drops of water! They can see objects that are up to 100 feet (30.5 m) away and hear sounds from more than 0.5 mile (0.8 km) away. Sharks can also sense vibrations, or small, quick movements, in the water around them.

In addition to these heightened senses, sharks have special organs that allow them to sense electrical fields given off by other living creatures. This allows sharks to find prey in dark or cloudy waters.

Sharks have eyes on the sides of their head. This gives them a wide range of vision, but they have a blind spot right in front of their nose.

A SHARK'S BITE

Sharks are top predators in the ocean food chain. Some sharks are famous for their rows and rows of sharp teeth. Sharks grow and lose thousands of teeth over a lifetime.

Sharks use their teeth to grasp slippery prey. They don't chew their meals but do sometimes rip them into smaller chunks. Sharks are curious and have been known to take "test bites" of things around them. If a shark bites a human, it will often release the person after one bite. This is because people don't have enough fat, which is the shark's favorite meal.

A great white shark's mouth is lined with up to 300 teeth in several rows.

19

FACE-OFF!

Late at night, an octopus hides, camouflaged to perfectly match the color and texture of the coral and plants surrounding it. A shark swims through the water. It's ready to sense the slightest movement or scent nearby.

Both octopuses and sharks can swim at speeds of up to 25 miles (40.2 km) per hour.

The octopus moves toward the shark, wrapping its tentacles tightly around the shark's body. The shark twists about, turning its head to sink its teeth into the octopus's soft body. The octopus releases ink, making it impossible for the shark to see. It bites the shark with its beak, releasing its venom. Who will win this fight to the death?

21

TEAM SHARK VS. TEAM OCTOPUS

With their many special skills, sharks and octopuses are very evenly matched when they clash. Both animals are opportunistic eaters, which means they'll eat whatever food they're able to find.

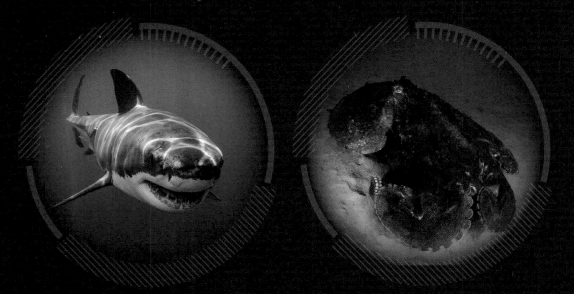

There have been cases of sharks eating octopuses and octopuses eating sharks, and it's difficult to say with certainty who the winner will be when the two face off. Which animal would you choose in the battle for survival? Would it be the crafty octopus with its entangling tentacles? Or would it be the fierce shark with its deadly bite?

GLOSSARY

behavior: The way a person or animal acts.

camouflage: Colors or shapes on animals that allow them to blend in with their surroundings.

communicate: To share ideas and feelings through sounds, motions, or actions.

entangle: To catch and wrap up tightly.

environment: The conditions that surround a living thing and affect the way it lives.

fossil: The preserved remains or impression of a plant or animal that died long ago.

gill: The body part that animals such as fish use to breathe in water.

nerves: Bunches of fibers that carry messages between the brain and other parts of the body.

prey: An animal hunted by other animals for food.

propel: To push or drive something forward or in another direction.

texture: The feel of a surface or object.

venom: A type of poison made by an animal and passed to another animal by a sting or bite.

INDEX

WEBSITES

Due to the changing nature of Internet links, PowerKids Press has developed an online list of websites related to the subject of this book. This site is updated regularly. Please use this link to access the list: www.powerkidslinks.com/handh/sharks